4th EDITION

The "EASY WAY" Series

EASY DOS IT!

by Ron Bauer

Illustrated by Sandra Kort

published by

the **EASY WAY PRESS**, inc.
ELECTRONIC PUBLISHERS

P.O. Box 906 ✦ Rochester, MI 48308-0906
Phone: (313) 651 - 9405

Easy DOS It!
Fourth Edition

TRADEMARK ACKNOWLEDGEMENTS:

IBM is a trademark of International Business Machines Corp.
Leading Edge is a trademark of Leading Edge Products, Inc.
Compaq is a trademark of Compaq Computer Corp.
Macintosh is a trademark of Apple Computer, Inc.
LaserWriter is a trademark of Apple Computer, Inc.
Word is a trademark of Microsoft
WordStar is a trademark of Micropro
Framework is a trademark of Ashton-Tate
MS-DOS is a trademark of Microsoft
PC-DOS is a trademark of IBM
PageMaker is a trademark of Aldus Corp.
MaxThink is a trademark of MaxThink, Inc.
Flight Simulator is a trademark of Microsoft
Sentinel is a trademark of Sentinel Technologies
PC to MAC and BACK is a trademark of dilithium Press

This booklet was written using Microsoft Word
Text was transferred from a Compaq using PC to MAC and BACK
The illustrations were produced using Macintosh software
Layout produced with PageMaker
Ready-for-camera printed with Apple LaserWriter

Library of Congress Cataloging-in-Publication Data

Bauer, Ron, 1938-
       Easy DOS it!

      ("The Learn in a day way!" series)
      1. PC DOS (Computer operating system) 2. MS-DOS
(Computer operating system) I. Title. II. Title: Easy
does it! III. Series.
QA76.76.063B39 1988   005.4'469   88-31079
ISBN 0-942019-04-0

Manufactured in the United States of America

for
Augie

☞CONTENTS

? WHY *DOS* IT MATTER?

A little over two years ago, I gave in and decided to use a personal computer as a word processor. That's *all* I wanted it for, a word processor. The morning I arrived at the computer store to pick it up, Dave, my salesman, had the entire system plugged in and running.

"Sit down," Dave said, "and I'll get you started with DOS."

"Started with what?"

"DOS (pronounced DAWSS)!" he said, chuckling, "Computers don't work too well without DOS, you know!"

I *didn't* know, nor did I know what a DOS was.

"Hey! No problem." he said. "I'm going to get you going. The rest is in your DOS manual."

"Forget it. No technical manuals!" I said, making my stand clear.

"You've *got* to use DOS," he continued. "You know, it's the disk operating system. You know, for running your programs and booting up and making your backups. You know, stuff like that."

He didn't know that I didn't know. Until that moment, I didn't even know I didn't know!

I pleaded with him. "Please don't do this to me." I defied him. "No way am I getting into a lot of technology!"

Pleading. Defying. Nothing could overcome Dave's eloquently simple response. "You *gotta* use DOS, or your computer won't work."

And, that's it, friend reader. DOS, an acronym for Disk Operating System, connects your computer to data on disks. Disks contain programs. Disks store your work. DOS comes on a disk. You ignore DOS, and your computer ignores you!

Which brings us to this book. It's written for the personal computer user who has no interest in technology. Each chapter progressively explains what you need to know in simple language, with examples. In a single day — at your own rate — you can learn the routine and repetitive "Essential Eleven" DOS operations *necessary* to run a floppy disk personal computer!

Good old Dave could have saved me a whole lot of trouble and time by giving me a copy of this book! It just hadn't been written yet. Now it has.

Ron Bauer
November, 1986

1 *THE COMPUTER SYSTEM*

Personal Computer Perceptions

Some ads for personal computers, especially those on television, foster false and misleading perceptions. You know what I mean. Someone presses a key on a keyboard causing a computer to display screens full of words and numbers and animated graphs. Or, a teenager types a few code words, and gains access to the high school class records. And, lately, people seem able to use personal computers to illustrate and print books!

Although computers can help accomplish all these tasks, and a few more, the process just isn't *that* easy. Nor is it particularly difficult. It's just that the common perception of a computer's capabilities is wrong.

A personal computer is, potentially, an easy to use TOOL. It can be as easy to use as a telephone, calculator, or typewriter. On second thought, it's *easier* to use than a typewriter!

A personal computer, by itself, though, is just a heap of HARDWARE...

> *HARDWARE*... *the machinery; the processor, drives, monitor, keyboard, printer, etc.*

The element that transforms a computer into a powerful, sophisticated and easy to use tool, capable of helping anyone do otherwise impossible things, is SOFTWARE...

> *SOFTWARE*... *the instructions for the hardware.*

All software originates from a keyboard. Hundreds, sometimes thousands, of keystrokes are necessary to make a computer draw graphs, communicate with other computers, or generate illustrations for a book.

How, then, do those people on TV do these things by pressing just one or two keys? Answer: The other keys are pressed in advance. Natural next question:

1

How does a person with no interest in technology learn to press those other keys? Welcome answer: No need to!

The mass of keystrokes – the software – the "technical stuff" – all is prepared by professionals, and distributed on DISKS...

> **DISKS**... *flat, circular pieces of mylar coated with magnetically sensitive material inside protective, plastic jackets.*

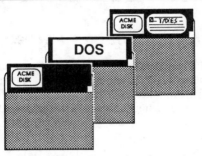

The software on a disk that puts a personal computer's power at the fingertips of non-technical person is called an APPLICATION PROGRAM...

> **APPLICATION PROGRAM**... *computer instructions packaged on a disk. Examples are word processors, data bases, spreadsheets, training packages, newsletter publishing templates, and games.*

Fewer people would shun the personal computer if they perceived this simple truth. It's merely an electronic tool operated from a keyboard, and all but the last few keystrokes necessary to instruct it come on disks called application programs.

Now that you have the correct perception, it's time to introduce you to the mechanism for getting the application programs from the disks and into the computer – DOS.

The Disk Operating System

The principle mechanism for using a personal computer is DOS...

> **DOS**... *the Disk Operating System. It's the software that instructs the computer how to interact with the disk drives, other hardware, and you.*

DOS transforms hardware and software into a computer system.

A Typical Computer System

The following illustration represents the generic computer system. It should give you an idea of how easy all this "advanced technology" can be. A wide variety of brands of hardware and types of software meet the criteria of this computer system...

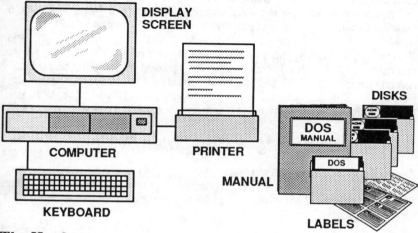

The Hardware

1. An IBM, or IBM-compatible, computer with at least one floppy disk drive

2. A keyboard

3. A color or monochrome monitor

4. A printer (dot matrix or other) with a supply of ribbons and paper

5. Appropriate cables to INTERFACE the hardware

This is the hardware you need for this book. You also need software.

The Software

1. The DOS disk and manual that come with the computer

2. Three blank floppy disks to match the drive

3. Labels, write protect tabs, and a marker (not a ball point)

I confess to sneaking in some computerese without a definition, the word INTERFACE...

INTERFACE... *(noun) a connection. (verb) to connect. For all practical purposes, these definitions are perfect.*

By the way, I hope you like the little definition boxes. I do. I think they cut down on the reading necessary to quickly absorb these ideas. I *know* they help me define important terms, many of which are in computerese (a term needing no definition).

Using computerese can't be avoided. It's too late. For years computerese has been creeping into our common conversation. You can try to resist, but it's futile. For example, I use the word *interface* every chance I get. I can't help myself. Eventually, some computerese will stick to you, too.

Computerese or not, by the time you reach the end of this book, to most people unfamiliar with this technology, you'll sound like a "computer whiz." Already a word like DOS seems almost natural, right? Okay, maybe not yet. No matter. You're stuck with this word because, like I said before, DOS is the principle mechanism for using a personal computer.

Choosing A Computer System

As electronic devices get *better*, their prices get *lower*. Computers, like every electronic device, are improved before the production models reach the market. Because of this rapid technological progress, they depreciate the moment they're purchased.

You can wait for that *better*, *lower-priced* version to come out. While you wait, though, you lose the benefits a computer can provide. You can buy an off-brand, "cheaper" computer. Then you're limited to few software choices.

What's the answer? Buy a computer that offers the widest variety of application programs. This way you get more use from your investment. Then, even though its resale value is lousy, you can make or save more money than you paid out. If you can manage that, your computer system is — *free*!

IBM PC Compatibles

Since the best "money deal" depends on the variety of available application programs (not counting games), the hardware most cost effective is either IBM, or IBM-COMPATIBLE...

> *IBM-COMPATIBLE... is any computer that's not an IBM, but uses a DOS that will run any software programs that run on an IBM computer.*

If you're puzzled about available application programs, do what I did. Become a reader of labels.

Read Labels

I read labels. I read advertising and reviews, too, but try not to take either seriously.

Labels, however, help you learn what *really* works with what. Don't be concerned if, initially, you don't understand most of what you're reading because you'll most likely be reading labels in a store. Right? So, ask questions. Get demonstrations.

One hint is to read the MINIMUM HARDWARE REQUIREMENTS on the labels of best selling software. Soon, you'll come to realize two related marketing facts that control the prices of computers...

1. Software *needs* determine hardware *choices*.

2. Hardware design determines which software you can use.

Keep an eye on "versions" and copyright dates, too. Sometimes one change by a major hardware or software manufacturer can render obsolete many of the "best bargains" of hardware or software.

Trends

The trend toward competition and standardization not only makes this learning what works with what easier, it also means a wider variety of application software is becoming available. Wider variety of software makes a personal computer more valuable. Today, you can find a program for almost any application. That virtually guarantees you can get maximum use from a personal computer without *ever* learning to PROGRAM...

PROGRAM (verb)... *to define and list the technical instructions for a computer to accomplish a specific task.*

Programming requires a knowledge of BASIC, PASCAL, COBOL, C, or some other technical language. Since so many applications are already being manufactured, all the programming you'll ever *need* is a matter of MEMORY, the type of memory unique to computer technology, and the subject of the next chapter.

(this page is almost blank)

2 *MEMORY*

Dynamic and Static Memory

Any discussion of memory related to computers invariably leads to major computerese. And, since the concept of computerese conflicts with the spirit of a book boldly asserting "easy" on its cover, I've limited the types of memory to be discussed to only two categories, DYNAMIC and STATIC.

DYNAMIC memory changes and moves in time and is temporary. STATIC memory, also called MASS STORAGE, doesn't change and is independent of time.

Before proceeding, a few clarifications are in order. Pay particular attention to the interchangeability of the terms *memory* and *storage*. Memory IS storage. Storage IS memory. Both are for retaining DATA...

> **DATA...** *a catch-all term meaning words, numbers, symbols, graphics, photos, sounds, etc.*

Computer memory makes it possible to gather, sort, modify, retrieve, and store data for short or long intervals. I think "storing data" sounds much better than "storing storage" or "storing memory." Don't you?

An Easy Review

Now, it might sound suspiciously like I'm moving toward embracing the jargon of the technicians. In a way I am. But, just some of it. After all, computers *are* technical. And, fortunately, most of the technical ideas you need to know are easy to understand. For example, in less than two chapters, you've already learned *four* technical ideas...

1. It takes both hardware and software to make a computer system.

2. The principle mechanism for using a personal computer is DOS which means disk operating system.

3. Data is stored in memory.

4. Memory and storage are analogous terms.

Okay so far? Of course you are.

The Static Memory

With STATIC memory, you remove or add data, but the data doesn't change, nor does it affect other data. Imagine slipping printed sheets of paper into file folders. The print on the sheets remains unchanged.

Let's begin our discussion of computer memory with DISK FILES...

DISK FILES... *groups of data recorded on a disk.*

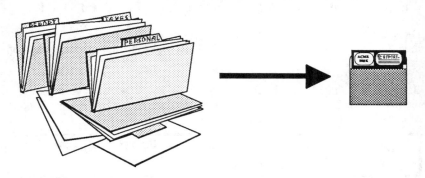

The term "file" is a good metaphor for STATIC memory. The image of a file folder is an easier concept to grasp than digital electronics.

The Dynamic Memory

DYNAMIC memory differs from static in two ways. First, it exists only when the computer system is active. Second, data added to it can interact with other data.

The easiest *analogy* I can concoct to illustrate the difference between static and dynamic memory is a comparison of a story in a book and one recited to an audience. A story in a book is static. Regardless of any reactions by the reader, the story in the book remains the same. As a story is recited to an audience, however, spontaneous reactions cause the story teller to make appropriate adjustments while reciting. The story is changed in one or more ways.

The principle DYNAMIC memory in a computer is RAM. RAM is an acronym for Random Access Memory. Most people gauge a computer's power by the capacity of its RAM to store BYTES...

BYTE... *is an alphanumeric character, a symbol, or a space. One byte equals eight BITS. A BIT is a BInary digiT. (You don't need all this information to use a computer.)*

Bytes are counted by thousands when measuring computer memory capacity. A kilobyte is a thousand bytes. The prefix "kilo" means a thousand, the letter k symbolizing a kilobyte. For example, a computer with 64k of RAM has one-tenth the power of a computer with 640k of RAM.

IRRELEVANT TECHNICAL NOTE

The "computer kilo" is 1024. That means 64 kilobytes is actually 65,536 bytes. Unless you're a technician, don't worry about this discrepancy. Stick with the rounded value.

There's one special DYNAMIC memory you'll hear about, but need not study. It's called ROM...

ROM... *is Read Only Memory, an electronic memory built into the computer. It retains data even when the computer is turned off.*

I have no useful comments about ROM, except that it provides special instructions to the computer's CPU...

CPU... *is the Central Processing Unit. It's the computer's main brain.*

PROCESSING (verb)... *sorting and arranging electronic data according to special instructions called PROGRAMS.*

PROGRAMS (noun)... *instructions for running a computer to accomplish one or more tasks.*

Wow! I got carried away with the definitions. Possibly, though, you already knew or had a good idea of the meanings of these terms before you ever saw this book. But, since each is important to this study, I wanted to make sure.

More Computerese

INPUT and OUTPUT are interchangeably used as nouns or verbs which qualifies them as computerese. Read the following paragraph to see what I mean...

RAM can accept various types and amounts of *input*, at varying times. You can *input* part or all related data until ready to *output*. In some situations, RAM can remember an entire program while simultaneously dealing with both *input* and *output*.

Of course it can, and does! So do you. If you're not sure, though, study the following illustration as you read on...

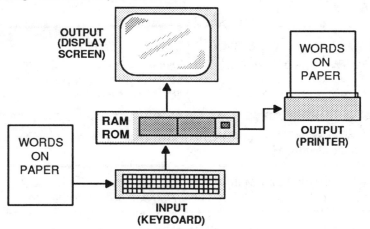

A typical input to output sequence can begin by copying words from a piece of paper — a medium of mass storage. Enter the words into the RAM of the computer using the keyboard. Immediately, you see one output of the RAM echoed on the display screen. Then, you can use another output device, the printer, to store the words on paper, as I said before, a medium of mass storage.

Mass storage, static memory is essential. One reason is that dynamic memory, RAM, needs a steady supply of electric current, or it can suddenly forget everything it knows!

The only problem with printed output as mass storage is that its data must be laboriously retyped to put it back into the computer. Not so with the mass storage efficiency of the DISK — the subject of the next chapter.

𝟛 *FLOPPY DISKS*

The Floppy Memory

The most-used medium of static memory for personal computers is the disk.
Application programs are stored on disks. You store your work on disks.
The most common type of disk is the FLOPPY DISK.

Anatomy Of A Floppy Disk

A floppy disk is a flat, circular piece of mylar coated with magnetically sensitive material. It's permanently sealed inside a 5.25" square protective, plastic
jacket. The entire assembly fits in an envelope made of paper, card, or plastic.

Several types are available including mini floppy, micro floppy, and high
density versions of each.

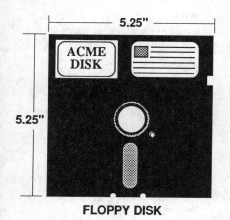

FLOPPY DISK

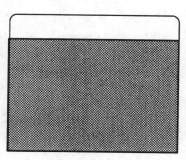

ENVELOPE

The floppy disk's plastic jacket has a label and special openings. In the next
chapter I'll explain the purpose of these openings.

For now, though, I'll tell you what's inside the jacket (DON'T OPEN YOURS!). It's the actual floppy disk, a flat, circular piece of mylar coated with magnetically sensitive material.

Also inside the jacket is a lining to help keep the disk clean.

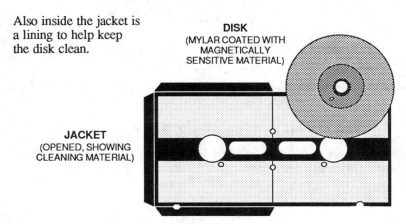

DISK
(MYLAR COATED WITH MAGNETICALLY SENSITIVE MATERIAL)

JACKET
(OPENED, SHOWING CLEANING MATERIAL)

The 3.5" Micro Floppy Disk

With the introduction of DOS 3.2, you can use 3.5" disks and drives as mass storage. Micro floppy disks and drives are used in laptop computers. The data on a micro floppy is compatible with that on a standard floppy disk.

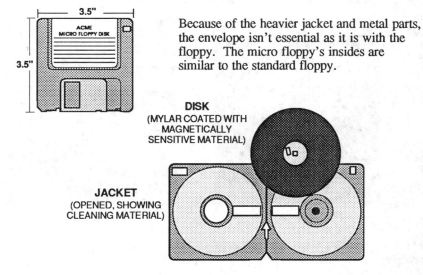

Because of the heavier jacket and metal parts, the envelope isn't essential as it is with the floppy. The micro floppy's insides are similar to the standard floppy.

DISK
(MYLAR COATED WITH MAGNETICALLY SENSITIVE MATERIAL)

JACKET
(OPENED, SHOWING CLEANING MATERIAL)

There's nothing more you need to know about the inside of the disks. So for the next several paragraphs, let's *stick* with the labels.

Labels provide information about the disk, or the files on the disks. Disks have three types of labels...

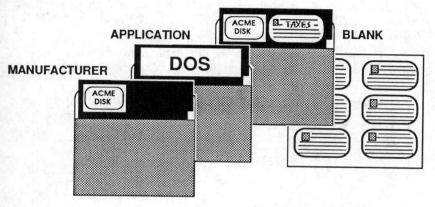

The Manufacturer's Label

First is the manufacturer's label. It tells you the capacity, type, and quality of the floppy. A double-sided, double-density floppy disk can store 360 kilobytes of data. That's approximately 200-250 typewritten, double-spaced, 8.5" by 11" pages. (More about disk capacities at the end of this chapter.)

How do you buy the *right* type and capacity disks for your system? Easy. Your computer manual tells you. Compare the specifications in your manual with those on the disk label (or box). Especially check this information before you buy any disks at "special prices."

Quality is important. The better the quality, the less chance of data errors. At least buy disks that have labels, and come in marked boxes!

The Application Label

The second type of label comes on disks containing commercial application programs. These labels range from plain to full-color with logos and illustrations. An example of a commercial application program label is your DOS label.

The Blank Label

Third are the blank labels. Several sheets of blank labels come with a box of disks. Or, you can buy them separately. You fill them in as needed. Floppy disks would all look alike if it weren't for labels. Without labels, you could misplace data.

Labelling Your Disks

Whenever possible, fill in labels before you stick them on disks. If you must write on a label while on a disk, USE A FELT TIP PEN, NEVER A BALL POINT. Pressure may *dent* the floppy and damage it.

When you put a label on a disk, slip the disk partly from its envelope to make room for the label, and to avoid touching the vulnerable surface.

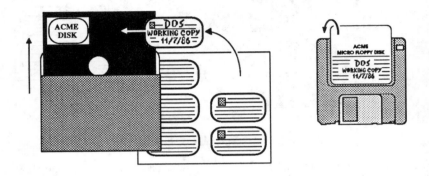

Floppy Precautions

Never touch any exposed surface of a floppy. Touching transfers body oil which will "glue" dust particles onto the mylar surface. Floppy disks are vulnerable. Besides not liking to be touched, they don't like to be bent, wet, heated, or dirtied.

Especially, never leave disks near magnetic fields which can be anything from a magnetized paper clip to a telephone receiver.

And, always return a floppy to its envelope when not using it. Then, put it in a box.

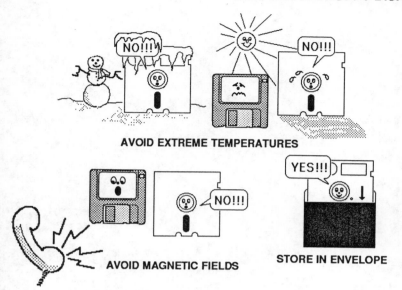

AVOID EXTREME TEMPERATURES

AVOID MAGNETIC FIELDS

STORE IN ENVELOPE

Before you go to the next chapter, one final comment regarding electronic memory. RAM and floppy disks *are not* software. Software is the electronic instructions, the files of data. The software can be moved from RAM to disk, disk to RAM, and disk to disk. To do it, you use DOS. DOS controls the disk drives, which are the subjects of the next chapter.

When accessing data, if DOS reaches the limits of RAM, it temporarily stores surplus data on a disk. This frees RAM to continue to interact with your input, the programming, and the CPU.

High Capacity Floppies

Some of the newer computer systems, such as the IBM PC AT and the PS/2 (Personal System/2) series, use "high capacity" floppy and micro floppy disks. These look like the standard disks. However, special processors and special drives are needed to take advantage of the greater capacities.

The high capacity floppy can store 1.2 megabytes (MEGA means million) of data. The high capacity micro floppy can hold 1.44 megabytes. The high capacity drives for these disks can read the standard capacity disks.

That's all I'll say about these in this book. Check the appropriate equipment operator manuals for more information.

(ditto)

FLOPPY DISK DRIVES

What Types of Drives?

As you recall from chapter one, the list of components of the "Typical Computer System" included one or more floppy disk drives. I didn't specify that these can be INTERNAL or EXTERNAL. Now I will.

A table-top computer can have either *internal*, *external*, or a combination of drives.

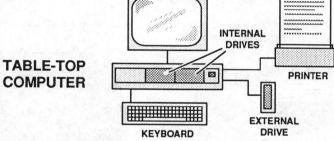

TABLE-TOP COMPUTER — INTERNAL DRIVES — PRINTER — KEYBOARD — EXTERNAL DRIVE

Portable and laptop computers invariably have *internal* drives. Although externals can be attached, the mobility is decreased.

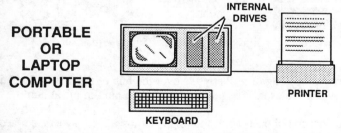

PORTABLE OR LAPTOP COMPUTER — INTERNAL DRIVES — PRINTER — KEYBOARD

Although the first illustration shows three drives, I won't discuss that combination in this book. I'll only cover two-drive systems. DOS doesn't mind if the two drives are internal or external, and neither do I. It doesn't matter if these drives are vertical or horizontal, either.

It *does* matter, though, that you correctly insert the floppies into floppy drives. No problem, really, as long as you rely on your right thumb.

THE THUMB

The Thumb

Whenever you remove a disk from its envelope, make it your habit to keep your thumb on the label.

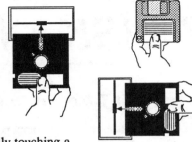

This is a good habit to develop. Always do it and you'll never insert a disk the wrong way. (Well, probably never.) You also reduce the risk of accidentally touching a floppy's magnetic surface through the openings in the jacket.

Disk Openings

The openings and notches in the plastic jacket of disks are for various mechanisms of the disk drives.

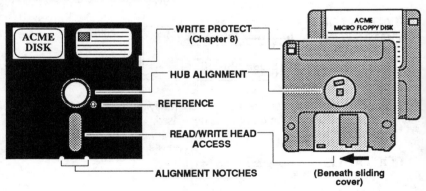

The central, round opening of a floppy fits over the hub of the drive. The hub aligns the disk and rotates it. The micro floppy has a built in metal hub.

The off-center, not-round opening of the floppy exposes the magnetic surface of the disk to the READ/WRITE HEAD. The micro floppy's opening is covered with a protective sliding cover.

The read/write head is to a disk what a phonograph needle is to a record. To read data is to "play it back." To write data is to... oops! This analogy just failed. That's the trouble with computerese. You see, *write* is analogous to *record*. If you could record onto a phongraph record, this would be a great analogy. Oh, well. You're probably way ahead of me by now on how the read/write head operates anyway. Check the following illustration to see.

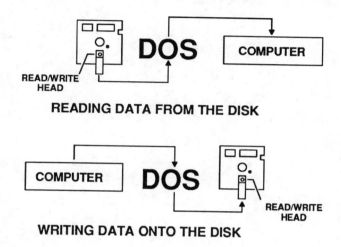

READING DATA FROM THE DISK

WRITING DATA ONTO THE DISK

Note that DOS is the intermediary in both reading and writing operations.

Various notches and holes in the jacket are for referencing and aligning the mylar disk to the read/write heads in the drive. The micro floppy handles these functions in a slightly different way. I don't think the details are important except to technical types.

Finally, there's the WRITE PROTECT system. I'll explain that in chapter eight.

(ditto)

5 *DOS*

As you now know, DOS is the *interface* (I TOLD you I use that word every chance I get!) between hardware and software. DOS makes it possible for you to connect your computer with your applications through the disk drives. Each time you use a personal computer, you must *program* it to run DOS because it's the disk operating system.

This is the easiest — probably the ONLY — technical stuff you'll ever need to know about programming a computer, though. And it's ridiculously easy to take care of because DOS does the work. All you do is enter a couple of simple, plain English commands which you'll get to try in the next chapter. Meanwhile, I want to tell you a few things about different versions of DOS.

Versions of DOS

This booklet covers versions of DOS higher than 2, that is 2.01, 2.02, 2.10, 2.11, 3.0, 3.1, etc. The wrong version of DOS can result in hardware and software problems.

DOS 1, for instance, will give you some trouble if you try to use DOS 2 disks. If, when using DOS 1, you come across a disk on which the contents are in the DOS 2 or 3 formats, you'll see gibberish or an error message on your screen.

Contrarily, if you use DOS 2 and 3, you'll have no trouble with DOS 1 disks. Newer versions of DOS are compatible with the older. That's because, fortunately for us, Microsoft, IBM, and accomplished software programmers are committed to standardization.

All example screens in this booklet are based on PC-DOS 3.1. If your screens differ slightly, it's because some manufacturers slightly vary their hardware design. They adjust their disk operating systems accordingly. But, you should have no problems. All essential commands will be there when you need them.

Which version of DOS do you have? It's printed on the label of your master DOS disk. (See *Check Your DOS Version* in the Addendum for another way to find out.)

Just for your reference, here's a brief list of the critical differences among versions of DOS, beginning in 1981...

- *1.0   This is the original version.*
- *1.1   Changed to accommodate double sided disks.*
- *2.0   Expanded for use of the multiple directories needed to organize hard disks.*
- *2.1   Modified to accommodate half height drives.*
- *3.0   Expanded to use high capacity floppies, the RAM disk, to LABEL volume names, and the ATTRIB command. The oddly named ATTRIB allows you to mark and unmark files making them "read-only." That means they can't be accidentally changed or erased while being used.*
- *3.1   Networking.*
- *3.2   Modified to accommodate 3.5" drives.*
- *3.3   Compatibility with PS/2 (Personal System/2) computers.*

PC or MS?

To be a proper intermediary between hardware and software, DOS must accommodate manufacturers' design differences. Making sure your applications match your system is another reason why you should read labels (I mentioned "label reading" in chapter one).

Labels of most current application programs say "Use PC-DOS 2.0 or higher." The PC stands for Personal Computer. PC-DOS is a slightly different version of MS-DOS. The MS in MS-DOS stands for Microsoft, the company that developed it. MS-DOS is the standard disk operating system for more than fifty leading personal computers, including IBM. The differences are minor, and only matter to users in terms of compatibility.

The main marketing strategy of MS-DOS computer manufacturers is to be compatible with IBM. That is, they must use MS-DOS, but want to run any programs designed for PC-DOS. Most do a good job. Some, however, claim total IBM compatibility, but fall short of meeting that noble goal. When you see a too-good-to-be-true low price on an "IBM compatible," investigate before buying.

One easy test for IBM compatibility, especially graphics ability, is to run a program called FLIGHT SIMULATOR, a remarkable interactive simulation of piloting an airplane which comes close to being more than a game. If the hardware can run this, it's probably compatible.

Your DOS

Your master DOS disk comes with a manual that describes more than thirty commands. It's a comprehensive REFERENCE that most people find incomprehensible.

I weeded out two-thirds of the commands because you'll probably never, or only rarely, need them. If you do, look them up in the DOS manual. For instance, you may occasionally choose to face a few of the DOS UTILITY PROGRAMS.

DOS Utility Programs

Utility programs are instructions to simplify routine or repetitious operations. Examples: SORT, PRINT, BUFFER, ECHO, ATTRIB, TREE, VOLUME, BASIC, and EDLIN.

I don't need these, and I work with computers and sophisticated software every day! I don't think you'll need them, either. The two I especially doubt you'll ever need are BASIC and EDLIN.

BASIC and EDLIN

BASIC is a programming language. I don't use it because I prefer to use application programs devised and written by someone else.

EDLIN is a "line editor." A line editor is as spartan a word processing program as you'll ever see. It's so simple, it's difficult to use! By the way, do you know the origin of the name, EDLIN? The ED is from EDitor, the LIN is from LINe. Clever? I don't think so, either.

BASIC and EDLIN are for programmers who use them to manipulate their machines in an eye-opening variety of ways. And I'm happy that the programmers program because I profit from their expert work.

DOS Details

As far as we nonprogrammers are concerned, the technical *details* of DOS matter little. Simply accept the fact that DOS, the disk operating system, through the use of a few commands, takes care of technical computer operations for you. It leaves you free to concentrate on your work.

Internal or External

INTERNAL commands automatically load into RAM when you boot the computer. They're *inside* the computer. These commands are always available at the system prompt. Internal is also called MEMORY RESIDENT.

EXTERNAL commands are *outside* the computer — on the DOS disk. To use these commands from the system prompt, the DOS disk must be in a drive.

Now see how easy DOS is...

# THE BOOT

Who Uses Bootstraps Anymore?

Guess what BOOT A COMPUTER means? No, it doesn't mean to kick it. Give up? It means to load the DOS instructions into the computer's memory!

Why the term BOOT? I've heard it's short for BOOTSTRAPS, as in the *well known* phrase "pulling up by bootstraps." How does this odd choice of a word relate to computers? I don't know.

I don't know why the two types of BOOT each have equally odd names, either. One's called COLD; the other's WARM. The odd thing is why not COLD and HOT, or WARM and COOL?

This chapter doesn't reveal the origin of this cryptic computerese. Someday it may be replaced with the more descriptive SYSTEM LOAD or SYSTEM RESET. Nah. BOOT isn't going away, so, we may as well get on with doing it.

The Cold Boot

First, let's do the COLD BOOT. A cold boot is only possible when a computer's switched off. (The computer's *off*, so it must be *cold!* Hmm. Could this be a clue?) With your DOS disk in the A: drive, close the door, then switch on the computer hardware.

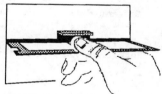

Watch and listen. As the hardware *warms up*, several things happen. In the first few seconds, the computer checks itself and gets its ROM and RAM organized. Then you hear and see "technical things." The fan starts. The indicator light on the A: drive glows bright red, alerting you that it's turning. The internal speaker beeps, and the printer expresses its readiness with a zip and a clunk. Then, on the monitor screen, you see the CURSOR...

> **CURSOR**... *a blinking, character-size line or block, on the monitor screen. Whenever you're puzzled with a computer display, find the cursor. It shows the location of the current action.*

You may see some other words and numbers on the screen, too. Soon, though, DOS completes the check of your system, leaving in its wake the first PROMPT...

> **PROMPT...** *suggested (sometimes a request for) information or next action.*

DOS's first prompt is for the "current DATE," and the screen looks like this...

```
Current date is Tue  1-01-1980
Enter new date (mm-dd-yy) : _
```

The date must be typed in a format acceptable to DOS. If you do it wrong, you get an error message. For example, type **XXX** at the cursor...

```
Current date is Tue  1-01-1980
Enter new date (mm-dd-yy) : XXX
```

Anything you type must be *entered* into the computer giving you a chance to check your typing before you make a final decision. In this case, exact typing isn't critical, so, press the [ENTER], or [RETURN], key...

```
Current date is Tue  1-01-1980
Enter new date (mm-dd-yy) : XXX

Invalid date
Enter new date (mm-dd-yy) :_
```

DOS politely informs you of your mistake. Type the correct current date at the cursor following the example format shown in parentheses (month-day-year). November 7, 1986 would be 11-7-1986. DOS accepts slashes (11/7/1986), too. If you're lazy, you can skip the "19." I always do. Once you've typed in the current date, press the [ENTER] key...

```
Current date is Tue  1-01-1980
Enter new date (mm-dd-yy) : XXX

Invalid date
Enter new date (mm-dd-yy) : 11/7/86_
```

If you make a typing error, use the BACKSPACE key to erase it, then retype. DOS will wait patiently until you're ready. Once the date is entered, you'll see the "current TIME" prompt...

```
Current date is Tue  1-01-1980
Enter new date (mm-dd-yy) : XXX_

Invalid date
Enter new date (mm-dd-yy) : 11/7/86
Current time is  0:01:34.16
Enter new time: _
```

The time must be in a format acceptable to DOS, too. DOS uses a 24 hour clock. That means 3 am is 3:00, but 3 pm is 15:00. There's an example of the time format on the line above the cursor. This example time, like the example date in the first prompt, is a DEFAULT...

DEFAULT... *a suggested response, often a recommended likely choice or action. When options are available, and you do not choose one, the option DOS gives you is by DEFAULT. The way to accept a default is to press the [ENTER] key.*

In the example screen, the default is 0:01:34.16. DOS will begin clocking your work from the moment you press the [ENTER] key...

```
The IBM Personal Computer DOS
Version 3.10 (C) Copyright IBM Corp.  1981, 1985
                (C) Copyright Microsoft Corp.  1981, 1985

A> _
```

Whatever choice you make, you end up at the "title page" of the disk operating system. It shows the DOS brand name, version, and copyright.

By the way, some people rationalize that it's okay to skip entering the time. As you'll discover as you spend more time with your computer, entering the correct date and time will enhance your record keeping. Besides, while you're typing, the time probably changes anyway. You'll be happy to know that DOS will settle for just hours and minutes, separated by a colon. When I say this book makes DOS easy, I mean it.

If you have a BUILT IN calendar and clock, the defaults will be the CORRECT date and time.

The Logged Drive

DOS uses the A: drive as the LOGGED DRIVE...

LOGGED DRIVE... *the active drive; the drive that responds to commands.*

The A> and blinking cursor mean DOS is logged onto the A: drive. It also means you're "at the system prompt" and ready to work. You can get to the system prompt with the second method of booting, too. It's called the WARM BOOT.

The Warm Boot

The only difference between the cold and warm boots is the first step. The first step of the cold boot is to switch on the hardware. For the warm boot, the hardware's already switched on, so you must press some keys.

Look at the keyboard, and locate the CONTROL, ALTERNATE, and DELETE keys. These keys are abbreviated: [CTRL], [ALT], and [DEL].

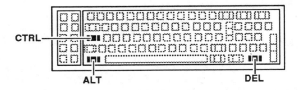

You must simultaneously press these keys. Press the [CTRL] and [ALT] keys with your left thumb and forefinger. Then, while holding them down, press the [DEL] key with your right forefinger.

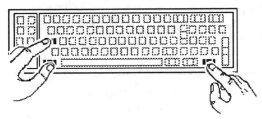

The monitor screen immediately goes blank, and the computer repeats the same ritual it performed with the cold boot except that the fan's already running. Like the first time, you eventually see the cursor, soon followed by the current date prompt. Enter the date and time as you did before to get to the system prompt.

Remember, whenever you see the A> and blinking cursor, you're at the prompt for the system — the Disk Operating System. This is the official DOS starting point. It confirms that the operating system is ready to respond to your commands.

If you're booting a computer with a version of DOS other than the one in our illustrations, the DOS title page will be slightly different. But, the system prompt will *still* be...

"THE SIGN OF THE DOS"

Get used to it.

An Easy Experiment

Sooner or later you'll want to change the system's DATE or TIME or both. Here's how to do it. Type **DATE**...

```
A>DATE_
```

When you type letters, you may use upper or lower-case. DOS doesn't know the difference.

Then, press the **[ENTER]** key...

```
Current date is Fri 11-7-1986
Enter new date (mm-dd-yy): _
```

Surprise! The current date prompt is back. Enter **6/1/99**, then press the **[ENTER]** key to reach the system prompt. You've changed the date in the computer's calendar. It's changed whether you have a built in calendar or not. Go ahead and verify. As before, type **DATE**, and press the **[ENTER]** key...

```
A>DATE
Current date is Tue  6-01-1999
Enter new date (mm-dd-yy): _
```

Easy, huh? Now, change the date back to today. Go on, you can do it without my help.

Changing the time is just as easy. At the system prompt, type **TIME**, and press the **[ENTER]** key. Then, as before, follow the prompts. Don't forget to change back to the correct time when you've finished experimenting.

That's it for booting and two essential DOS commands, DATE and TIME. Now you're ready to look at the FILES.

(ditto)

7 LOOK AT THE FILES

The File Drawer Metaphor

As I explained in chapter two, the image of groups of data stored in a file
folder is an easier concept to grasp than digital electronics. To carry the
imagery further, the file drawer metaphor seems the easiest way to visualize
groups of files stored on a disk.

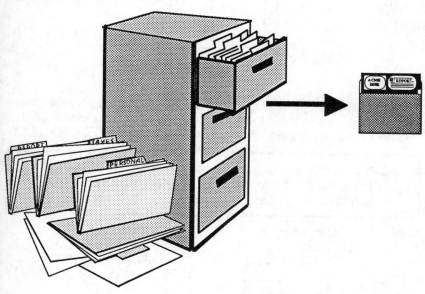

A disk, however, doesn't look like a file drawer. And, if you look at the disk
under a microscope you won't see tiny file folders in it. Since there are
actually no file folders, DOS provides other means to look into the electronic
file drawer, the DIR command.

The DIR Command

DIR stands for DIRectory. A DIRECTORY is a list of the files recorded on a disk. You can see the DIRECTORY with the DIR command. Type **DIR**, and watch your screen as you press the [**ENTER**] key...

```
FORMAT    COM      9398    3-07-85    1:43p
GRAFTABL  COM      1169    3-07-85    1:43p
GRAPHICS  COM      3111    3-07-85    1:43p
JOIN      EXE     15971    3-07-85    1:43p
KEYBFR    COM      2289    3-07-85    1:43p
KEYBGR    COM      2234    3-07-85    1:43p
KEYBIT    COM      2177    3-07-85    1:43p
KEYBSP    COM      2267    3-07-85    1:43p
KEYBUK    COM      2164    3-07-85    1:43p
LABEL     COM      1826    3-07-85    1:43p
MODE      COM      5295    3-07-85    1:43p
MORE      COM       282    3-07-85    1:43p
PRINT     COM      8291    3-07-85    1:43p
RECOVER   COM      4050    3-07-85    1:43p
RESTORE   COM      5410    3-07-85    1:43p
SELECT    COM      2084    3-07-85    1:43p
SHARE     EXE      8304    3-07-85    1:43p
SORT      EXE      1664    3-07-85    1:43p
SUBST     EXE     16611    3-07-85    1:43p
SYS       COM      3727    3-07-85    1:43p
TREE      COM      2831    3-07-85    1:43p
VDISK     SYS      3307    3-07-85    1:43p
        36 File(s)       61440 bytes free

A> _
```

The filenames went by fast, didn't they? You're already at the bottom of a directory of thirty-six (or whatever number are on your DOS disk) files, but only *twenty-two* are showing. What you just witnessed is called a SCROLL...

> **SCROLL**... *characters move on a screen. The easiest way to understand scrolling is to imagine your screen's a window. You see only the data that passes the window.*

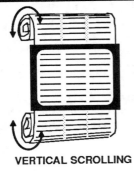

VERTICAL SCROLLING

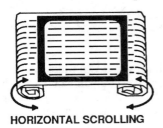

HORIZONTAL SCROLLING

Scrolling is fast, but you don't need to sign up for a speed reading course. There are easier ways. One is to manually STOP the scroll; the other is to have DOS automatically PAUSE it.

How To Stop and Pause

To manually STOP the scroll, it's necessary to temporarily change the meaning of the S key on the keyboard. How? With a *special* key.

An example of a *special* key is the [SHIFT] key on a typewriter. You use the [SHIFT] key to change between upper and lower case letters, or numbers and symbols.

A computer keyboard has a [SHIFT], and other *special* keys, too. Three special keys are [CTRL], [ALT], and [DEL]. In the previous chapter, you used all three to warm boot.

This time, you combine the [CTRL] key with a letter key. The [CTRL] key combined with the S key means STOP. Type **DIR**, and press the [ENTER] key. Once the directory is scrolling, press the [CTRL] key, then, while holding it down, press the S key.

If you were quick enough, the scrolling stopped. Isn't that easy? It's easy to start scrolling again, too, because you use the same command. [CTRL] S stops or starts scrolling. Go ahead and start again. And, if you're really quick, you can stop and start several times before the scrolling reaches the system prompt.

The second way to control scrolling takes less coordination. This time, you follow the DIR command with "/P." The /P stands for PAUSE. Type **DIR/P**, and press the [ENTER] key...

```
ANSI      SYS    1651   3-07-85   1:43p
ASSIGN    COM    1509   3-07-85   1:43p
ATTRIB    EXE   15091   3-07-85   1:43p
BACKUP    COM    5577   3-07-85   1:43p
BASIC     COM   17792   3-07-85   1:43p
BASICA    COM   27520   3-07-85   1:43p
CHKDSK    COM    9435   3-07-85   1:43p
COMMAND   COM   23210   3-07-85   1:43p
COMP      COM    3664   3-07-85   1:43p
DISKCOMP  COM    4073   3-07-85   1:43p
DISKCOPY  COM    4329   3-07-85   1:43p
EDLIN     COM    7261   3-07-85   1:43p
FDISK     COM    8173   3-07-85   1:43p
FIND      EXE    6403   3-07-85   1:43p
FORMAT    COM    9398   3-07-85   1:43p
GRAFTABL  COM    1169   3-07-85   1:43p
GRAPHICS  COM    3111   3-07-85   1:43p
JOIN      EXE   15971   3-07-85   1:43p
KEYBFR    COM    2289   3-07-85   1:43p
KEYBGR    COM    2234   3-07-85   1:43p
KEYBIT    COM    2177   3-07-85   1:43p
KEYBSP    COM    2267   3-07-85   1:43p
KEYBUK    COM    2164   3-07-85   1:43p
Strike a key when ready .  .  .
```

That's better, isn't it? The screen fills to the limit and pauses. The file at the top of the screen is the first in the directory. At the bottom of the screen is an instruction for continuing.

Pausing allows you to look at the names of all the files on the directory, one screen at a time. Probably, though, you'll find the [CTRL] S command becoming the most useful regardless of your coordination. Later in this book I'll show you other uses for it.

Meanwhile, let's take time out for some more computerese. This is a term that comes up again and again. It's PARAMETER...

> **PARAMETER...** *the instructions you type after a command.*

Parameters pop up throughout DOS. You just used one to pause the DIR display. That parameter is a SWITCH...

> **SWITCH...** *one type of parameter. A SWITCH is identified by a slash (/) followed by a letter or a number.*

DIR/P is a command with a switch. Another is DIR/W. You can switch the DIR command to list the files in a wide display by adding /W. Type **DIR/W**, then press the [ENTER] key...

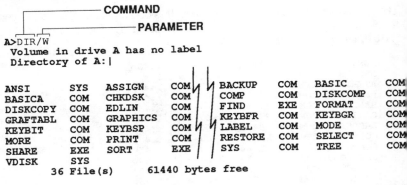

```
                      ┌─────── COMMAND
                      │  ┌──────── PARAMETER
                      │  │ │
A>DIR/W
  Volume in drive A has no label
  Directory of A:|

  ANSI      SYS   ASSIGN   COM    BACKUP    COM   BASIC      COM
  BASICA    COM   CHKDSK   COM    COMP      COM   DISKCOMP   COM
  DISKCOPY  COM   EDLIN    COM    FIND      EXE   FORMAT     COM
  GRAFTABL  COM   GRAPHICS COM    KEYBFR    COM   KEYBGR     COM
  KEYBIT    COM   KEYBSP   COM    LABEL     COM   MODE       COM
  MORE      COM   PRINT    COM    RESTORE   COM   SELECT     COM
  SHARE     EXE   SORT     EXE    SYS       COM   TREE       COM
  VDISK     SYS
         36 File(s)         61440 bytes free

A>_
```

I don't know if you counted the files. Probably not. If you did, though, you discovered that this directory shows more filenames per screen than does the DIR or DIR/P commands. Since *all* the files now fit on the screen, you may have noticed.

Later in this book, you'll learn several other useful switches.

The Five Columns

As you recall from the previous chapter, the standard DIR display shows files in five columns. These columns are: the filename, the extension, the size measured in bytes, and the date and time the file was recorded on the disk...

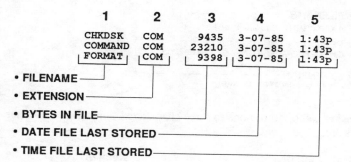

	1	2	3	4	5
	CHKDSK	COM	9435	3-07-85	1:43p
	COMMAND	COM	23210	3-07-85	1:43p
	FORMAT	COM	9398	3-07-85	1:43p

- FILENAME
- EXTENSION
- BYTES IN FILE
- DATE FILE LAST STORED
- TIME FILE LAST STORED

The first and second columns show the filenames and extension, if any. A filename is the name of the file, excluding the extension. Sometimes these names are in a shorthand or code. That's because filenames are limited to eight characters.

The characters can be letters, numbers, certain symbols, or any combination. Here are some examples of shortening the names of the files into filenames...

NAMES OF FILES	FILENAMES
FAMILY AND FRIENDS	FAMFRNDS
CLASSMATES	CLASSMTS
BOOK LIST ONE	BOOKS1
BOOK LIST TWO	BOOKS2
NEW LIST	NEWLIST
LIST A - M	LISTA-M
LIST N - Z	LISTN-Z
TO DO	TO_DO

Either upper- or lower-case letters work. Most symbols work. Spaces *don't* work. DOS uses spaces to distinguish the elements of a command request. SO, YOU CAN'T USE SPACES AS PART OF A FILENAME.

If you *must* use a filename with more than a single word, such as TO DO, then use the underline character in place of the space: like this TO_DO. Don't forget the eight character filename limit.

Don't use any punctuation in a filename except an underline or a hyphen.
Never use a period. A period marks the end of the filename and the beginning
of the extension. The period doesn't show up in a directory.

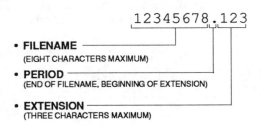

An extension can be from none to three characters. Some three character
examples are...

Function or Name	Related Extension
COMMAND	COM
EXECUTE	EXE
BATCH	BAT
TEXT	TXT
DOCUMENT	DOC
BACKUP	BAK
JANUARY	JAN
FEBRUARY	FEB
MARCH	MAR
ETCETERA	ETC

In DOS, most extensions show the function of the file. Most other programs
use descriptive extensions, too. Micropro's WordStar, uses the extension
TXT for TeXT files. Microsoft's Word uses DOC for DOCument files.
MaxThink uses none except for backup files which end with BAK for
BAcKup. But, since most applications use the extensions, I recommend you
don't.

Filename Precautions

There are certain specific character combinations in filenames (or extensions) to avoid, too. The following, for example, are reserved to identify certain computer devices...

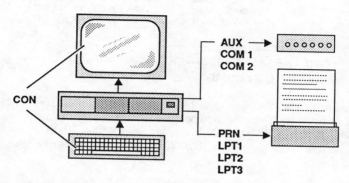

Avoid certain SYMBOLS. These symbols are okay to use...

> ! @ # $ % & ( ) _ - ' ` ~ "

But don't use...

> > < | ^ * ? \ /

The symbols to avoid have *special* functions which aren't covered in this chapter because the variations can lead to irrelevant complications. And this book is supposed to be EASY!

By now, you probably don't remember most of the symbols and special extensions you just read, anyway. That's fine. I don't remember most of them, either. That's why I follow the *Easy DOS It!* generic rules for filenames and extensions...

1. Use ONLY letters and numbers in filenames.

2. Don't use extensions unless related to the application.

The Last Three Columns

Here's one more look at part of a directory...

```
       1        2       3        4        5

    CHKDSK    COM    9435    3-07-85    1:43p
    COMMAND   COM   23210    3-07-85    1:43p
    FORMAT    COM    9398    3-07-85    1:43p
```

- BYTES IN FILE
- DATE FILE LAST STORED
- TIME FILE LAST STORED

Column three shows the number of bytes (chapter two) in the file. The number of bytes are, from the viewpoint of storage space, a relative value. For example, if "file X" has 2500 bytes, and "file Y" has 10,000 bytes, then "file Y" is four times bigger! A 360,000 byte disk can, in theory, store 36 files the size of "file Y."

DOS automatically updates the directory as you store, retrieve, and work with the files. Columns four and five show the date and time the file was last stored on the disk.

HARD DISK USERS
IMPORTANT!!!

That's it for filenames and extensions — unless your computer has a HARD DISK. If it does, use the **Hard DOS It!** book to continue.

8 PREPARE DISKS

Blank Disks

Blank disks are blank.

That's not so self-evident as it sounds. In computerese, disks are either...

1. Blank.

2. Blank, but formatted.

This is computerese because blank should be blank, and in this instance it isn't. But, let's not quibble. Let's investigate the differences.

DOS provides a command called FORMAT. Its function is to prepare disks to conform to your disk drives. Your disks must be prepared with this command before you can store files on them.

Jim Kelsh of Central Michigan University, a computer scientist, compares a computer to a child. He analogizes a blank disk to a blank sheet of paper; a formatted disk to a lined sheet of paper. The child needs the lines before he or she can begin to write (in a legible manner). Interesting.

Before I show you how to format blank disks for DOS, take the precaution to protect your master disk. Check that it's write protected.

Write Protect

When you write protect a disk, the read/write head can't write on it. A write protected disk is safe from accidental, or deliberate, erasure. The methods for write protecting floppy and micro floppy disks are slightly different, even though the purpose is the same.

Make sure your master DOS disk is write protected now. If it has an open write protect notch, the large notch at the edge of the disk near the label, wrap a self-adhesive write protect tab around it...

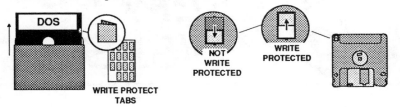

Micro floppy disks have built-in write protect tabs. Set the one on your master DOS disk in the OPEN position. When the tab's in the open position, the disk is write protected. It's the opposite of the floppy disk which is NOT write protected when the notch is open. (I wonder who made THAT decision?!)

The Two Drive System

The procedures to follow are patterned on a two floppy disk drive system. In this type of system, both drives are mechanically the same, but each has a different name. One's called the A: drive, the other is the B: drive. Note that each of the drive names includes a colon.

Without specific instructions, DOS will *only* use the DEFAULT DRIVE...

DEFAULT DRIVE... *the logged drive.*

Although it looks like I'm using one computerese term to define another, that's only because I am. Both terms were covered in chapter six, though, so they should be familiar. If not, review them now.

Here's some help. When you boot a computer, the A> prompt appears. Right? That means A: is the logged drive by default.

If you use the DIR command, *by default* you see the directory of the A: drive. This brings us to a question. How do you see the directory of the other drive?

The Other Drive

B: is the other drive. To gain access to its contents, there are two choices. One is to make the other drive the logged drive. Let's "log onto" it. Type **B:**, and press the [ENTER] key...

    A>B:

    B> _

As you can see, the system prompt changes to B>. The B: drive is now the logged drive. DOS will now look for data, such as a directory, on the disk in the B: drive.

Put your DOS disk in the B: drive, and close the door. Then type **DIR**, and press the **[ENTER]** key...

```
B>DIR
Volume in drive B has no label
Directory of B:\

ANSI      SYS      1651    3-07-85    1:43p
ASSIGN    COM      1509    3-07-85    1:43p
ATTRIB    EXE     15091    3-07-85    1:43p
BACKUP    COM      5577    3-07-85    1:43p
```

```
SUBST     EXE     16611    3-07-85    1:43p
SYS       COM      3727    3-07-85    1:43p
TREE      COM      2831    3-07-85    1:43p
VDISK     SYS      3307    3-07-85    1:43p
        36 File(s)        61440 bytes free

B> _
```

As you can see, the B: drive, the logged drive, is also the default. Log back onto the A: drive by reversing the previous procedure. Simply type **A:** and press the **[ENTER]** key.

Once the logged drive is again A:, you can use the second method of accessing the other drive. That method is to specify the other drive with a drive specifying parameter. Type **DIR B:**, and press the **[ENTER]** key...

```
                  ┌────── COMMAND
                  │  ┌─── PARAMETER
A>DIR B:
Volume in drive B has no label
Directory of B:\

ANSI      SYS      1651    3-07-85    1:43p
ASSIGN    COM      1509    3-07-85    1:43p
ATTRIB    EXE     15091    3-07-85    1:43p
BACKUP    COM      5577    3-07-85    1:43p
```

```
SUBST     EXE     16611    3-07-85    1:43p
SYS       COM      3727    3-07-85    1:43p
TREE      COM      2831    3-07-85    1:43p
VDISK     SYS      3307    3-07-85    1:43p
        36 File(s)        61440 bytes free

A> _
```

This time, using a parameter, you instructed DOS to act on the other drive, not the logged drive. This "command parameter" idea becomes easier to understand the more you use it. Parameters are particularly important when preparing disks, which you do with the FORMAT command.

The FORMAT Command

Blank disks must be prepared before they can hold files. The procedure for preparing a blank disk is to run the DOS program called FORMAT. FORMAT analyzes a disk for defective tracks, initializes a directory, sets up file allocations, and makes other technical modifications. DOS does it, not you. You do the easy part.

WARNING

If your computer has a hard disk (a C: drive), DON'T FORMAT IT! (Refer to **Hard DOS It!** *first.)*

Before you begin, though, prepare three labels. (Remember the precautions about labels in chapter three.) On one, print "BLANK FORMATTED." On the second, print "BLANK FORMATTED WITH SYSTEM." On the third, print "DOS/WORKING COPY." Put one label on each of the three blank disks mentioned in chapter one.

FORMAT erases everything on the disk. So, check the directory of any disk you suspect may contain some data before running FORMAT. Put the disk labelled "BLANK FORMATTED" in the A: drive, and close the door. Type **DIR**, and press the **[ENTER]** key...

```
A>DIR
Disk error reading in drive A
Abort, Retry, Ignore? _
```

The "disk error" message usually means there's no formatting. But, it *could* mean wrong formatting or a damaged disk. Lets assume the disk is blank. Type **A** for Abort, bringing you back to the system prompt.

A similar message to the above is...

```
Not ready error reading in drive A
Abort, Retry, Ignore? _
```

This message means you left the drive door open. Leaving a drive door open does no harm. Put things right by closing it, then press **R** for Retry.

WARNING

When the red light on a drive is glowing, the internal mechanisms of
the drive are active. WAIT UNTIL THE LIGHT GOES OFF before
touching the door, or removing or inserting a disk. If it doesn't go off
in one or two minutes, boot your computer again.

Swap the disks in the A: and B: drives. I know you know what that means,
but I'll explain anyway. Replace the disk in the A: drive with your DOS disk
(it should still be in the B: drive). Put the disk labelled "BLANK
FORMATTED" into the B: drive. Then, enter the FORMAT command by
typing **FORMAT B:**, and pressing the **[ENTER]** key...

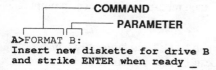

```
A>FORMAT B:
Insert new diskette for drive B
and strike ENTER when ready _
```

Once again, you use the drive specifying parameter. If you're ready, "strike
ENTER" which means the same as press the **[ENTER]** key...

```
Formatting...
```

Now you wait. (This technical stuff is tough!) While you're waiting, you can
take a stretch, look out the window, or, if your version of DOS shows it,
stare at the running Head/Cylinder count. DOS is doing all the work. When
the formatting is complete, you see...

```
Formatting...Format complete

        362496 bytes total disk space
        362496 bytes available on disk

Format another (Y/N)? _
```

Press **N** for *No*. Then press the **[ENTER]** key, leaving the FORMAT
program, and returning to the system prompt.

---

*It's possible that FORMAT may detect some errors. If it
does, you'll see a message telling you there are "bytes
in bad sectors." Try formatting again. If the bad sector
message is still there, I recommend you use a different
disk, or you may eventually have trouble.*

This disk is now considered "a blank, formatted disk" as opposed to "a blank disk." I'm still curious about this paradoxical use of the term blank. I can only suspect that the guy who came up with the term *boot* is involved. There's no way to prove it, though.

The directory of the blank, formatted disk differs from the directory of the blank disk. Type **DIR B:**, and press the [ENTER] key...

```
A>DIR B:
 Volume in drive B has no label
 Directory of B:\

File not found

A> _
```

As you can see, the "official" message shows that DOS now has something it can read. It reads and finds no files, then returns to the system prompt because everything's okay.

By the way, don't worry about "volume labels" and "directory names." This book makes DOS easy because it doesn't waste your time on irrelevant explanations. They're irrelevant when you're new to personal computing, and, probably, will stay that way! If you *want* more information, though, read your DOS manual.

Formatted With System

Replace the disk in the B: drive with the disk labelled "BLANK FORMATTED WITH SYSTEM." Close the door. This time type **FORMAT B:/S**, and press the [ENTER] key...

```
                 ┌─────── COMMAND
                 │   ┌────── PARAMETERS
         ┌────┐ ┌─┐
A>FORMAT B:/S
Insert new diskette for drive B:
and strike ENTER when ready _
```

Press (or strike) the [ENTER] key...

```
Formatting...Format complete

      362496 48960 bytes total disk space
      62464 bytes used by system
      300032 bytes available on disk

Format another? (Y/N)? _
```

Type **N**, and press the [ENTER] key to get back to the system prompt.

Note that the message now includes *"62464 bytes used by system."* By adding the /S switch parameter to the FORMAT command, a second parameter, you tell DOS to format the disk in the B: drive, and to copy certain files onto the disk once it's formatted.

This disk is called "blank," even though it's qualified to include certain files, a COMMAND.COM file and some "system files." If you look at the directory of this newly formatted disk, you'll see one file, the COMMAND.COM...

COMMAND.COM... *instructions to carry out DOS commands stored in RAM.*

The "system files" don't show up on the directory because they're hidden! Why are they hidden? I don't know. I do know you need them and the COMMAND.COM on a disk for it to boot your computer.

Since these files are critical, as are other DOS command files, you should definitely have a *duplicate* of the master DOS disk. You'd be in trouble if something happened to it because, as you've learned, DOS is the connection between hardware and software. There is a way to make an exact copy of the DOS disk. It's the DISKCOPY command.

The DISKCOPY Command

The DISKCOPY command reads ALL formatting and data from one disk, and writes, or copies, it onto another. It makes an *exact* copy.

The master DOS disk is in the A: drive. Replace the disk in the B: drive with the one labelled "DOS/WORKING COPY." Type **DISKCOPY A: B:,** then press the [**ENTER**] key...

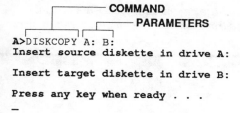

```
                    COMMAND
                        PARAMETERS
A>DISKCOPY A: B:
Insert source diskette in drive A:

Insert target diskette in drive B:

Press any key when ready . . .
-
```

This time there are two parameters. One to specify the source, the second to specify the target. Left to right, just like you read.

The instructions on your screen tell you what to do next. The disks (or "diskettes" as DOS so elegantly declares) are already in place. Press any key. You'll see both disk drive lights glowing at appropriate times and the following acknowledgement on the screen...

```
Copying 40 tracks
9 Sectors/Track, 2 side(s)
```

You can DISKCOPY onto a blank (unformatted) disk because DOS checks for correct formatting before it copies. If necessary, it formats it...

```
Formatting while copying
```

When the DISKCOPY procedure is complete, you'll see...

```
Copy another diskette (Y/N)? _
```

Press **N**, which brings you back to the system prompt. Don't remove the disks from their drives yet. This is one of those times when you want to make sure you have an EXACT copy. And, you can with the DISKCOMP command.

The DISKCOMP Command

DOS has a program for comparing every bit and byte of two disks. It's called DISKCOMP (DISK COMPare). DISKCOMP means disk comparison. You run DISKCOMP the same way you did DISKCOPY. Type **DISKCOMP A: B:**...

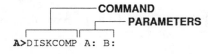

```
                    ┌──────── COMMAND
                    │   ┌──── PARAMETERS
      ┌─────────┐ ┌─┐┌─┐
      A>DISKCOMP A: B:
```

REMEMBER, when you use parameters, spaces are critical. Isolate drive specifiers from commands with appropriate spaces.

Press the [**ENTER**] key...

```
Insert FIRST diskette in drive A:

Insert SECOND diskette in drive B:

Press any key when ready . . .
_
```

They're in place, so press any key...

```
Comparing 40 tracks
9 sectors per track, 2 side(s)
```

Again the disk drives' lights will alternately glow as DOS compares the disks. When complete, the screen *should* say...

```
Compare OK
Compare another diskette (Y/N)? _
```

Press **N** to return to the system prompt.

> *If the disks don't compare ok, you didn't get an exact copy.*
> *Try DISKCOMP again with the same disk. If the procedure*
> *fails a second time, get a new blank disk, and repeat both*
> *the DISKCOPY and DISKCOMP procedures.*

Once you've completed preparing your new, perfect "DOS/WORKING COPY," take a look at it with the DIR command. (Type **DIR B:**, and press the **[ENTER]** key.) The directory should match that of the master DOS disk.

When you're satisfied, remove the master DOS disk from the A: drive, and put it in a secure place. Remove the "DOS/WORKING COPY" disk (from now on I'll call it the DOS disk) from the B: drive. Put it in the A: drive, and close the door.

> *REMINDER... When you use the FORMAT or DISKCOPY*
> *commands, always be cautious. You can easily destroy*
> *important files. Check first.*

One Floppy Drive Only

If you don't specify the drives, DOS will carry out DISKCOPY, DISKCOMP, and FORMAT operations on just one drive, the logged drive. It's the same if you only have one drive.

One drive, however, requires disk swapping. By disk swapping, I mean you must swap disks back and forth during the command processes. Fortunately, DOS provides step-by-step instruction messages on the screen to make it easy.

47

(ditto)

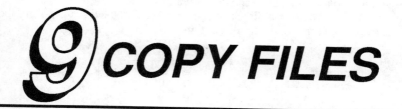

COPY FILES

The Longest Chapter

This is the longest chapter in this book. Does that mean it's jammed with commands to learn? No. Actually, there's only *one* command to learn, but it's pivotal. It's also economical. When you learn to use it, you simultaneously learn three others. That's four for the price of one!

The pivotal command is COPY. The bargain three are DIR, RENAME (REN), and ERASE (DEL). True, you've already used DIR in chapters seven and eight. Now, though, you'll learn several power features and functional shortcuts it shares with the others.

DON'T SKIP THROUGH THIS CHAPTER BECAUSE OF ITS LENGTH. Try *all* the examples at least once, and try them *in order*. The progression will help you *understand* important relationships. Understanding is preferable to remembering. If you understand, you can usually reconstruct what you forget.

The COPY Command

COPY differs from DISKCOPY (chapter eight) in that...

COPY	DISKCOPY
Copies only files.	Copies all contents of a disk.
Copies files into available space.	Wipes out anything on the target disk.
Copies only onto formatted disks.	Formats blank disks.

Try out the COPY command by copying a file from the DOS disk in the A: drive onto a disk in the B: drive. If you're picking up where you left off in the previous chapter, your DOS disk is in place, but you must replace the disk in the B: drive. Put the disk labelled "BLANK FORMATTED" into the B: drive. Then, at the system prompt, type **COPY A:COMMAND.COM B:**, and press the **[ENTER]** key...

```
A>COPY A:COMMAND.COM B:
      1 File(s) copied

A> _
```

This time you specified both drives, but in a different way. In chapter eight, I told you to "isolate commands and drives with spaces." That's still true. But don't put a space between a drive and filename because the drive *is part of* the filename. Look at the following illustration...

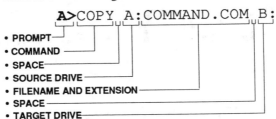

A space is between the filename's extension, if there is one, and the target drive parameter. Look at the illustration again. This is the result of the rule that a space precedes a drive specifier.

Okay, now back to the COPY command. Look at the directory of the disk in the B: drive to see if the copy arrived. Type **DIR B:**, and press the **[ENTER]** key...

```
A>DIR B:

    Volume in drive B has no label
    Directory of B:\

COMMAND   COM     23210   3-07-85   1:43p

A>_
```

This is the file you copied. It's there on the B: drive, so you must have specified the drive parameter the right way, and in the correct order.

Parameter Priority

The priority of parameters is *source* to *target*. It parallels the order in which DOS executes operations. For example, you just instructed DOS to copy a file from the disk in the A: drive onto the disk in the B: drive.

To copy in the opposite direction, type **COPY B:COMMAND.COM A:**, and press the **[ENTER]** key...

```
A>COPY B:COMMAND.COM A:
        1 File(s) copied

A> _
```

Okay. Copying one file either way is easy. Sometimes, though, it's necessary to copy a *long* list of files. This could entail tedious typing if it weren't for WILD CARDS!

Wild Card Characters

DOS provides two "wild card" characters that can represent any or all characters of filenames and extensions.

The first is the * (asterisk) which can represent up to all eight filename characters, or up to all three extension characters. For example, one * (asterisk) before and another after a period represents all the files on a disk.

Using that idea, here's how to copy all the files from the DOS disk onto the disk in the B: drive. Type **COPY A:*.* B:**...

```
            A>COPY A:*.* B:
• ALL FILENAMES ─────────────────┘   │
• ALL EXTENSIONS─────────────────────┘
```

Watch the screen as you press the **[ENTER]** key...

```
A>COPY A:*.* B:
A:ANSI.SYS
A:ASSIGN.COM
A:ATTRIB.EXE
A:BACKUP.COM
A:BASIC.COM
A:BASICA.COM



A:SHARE.EXE
A:SORT.EXE
A:SUBST.EXE
A:SYS.COM
A:TREE.COM
A:VDISK.SYS
        36 File(s) copied

A>_
```

The Hidden System Files

Actually, not *all* the files are copied. The "hidden" system files, which I briefly mentioned in chapter eight, aren't covered by the wild card characters, or the COPY command, for that matter.

To make sense of this, let's do some detective work. Our assignment is to prove the hidden files exist. We'll use a simple experiment and a little deductive reasoning.

Replace the disk in the B: drive with the disk labelled "BLANK FORMATTED WITH SYSTEM." Copy all the files from the DOS disk onto it, using the wild card characters. Then compare the directories of these disks.

HINT... Use the commands COPY A:*.* B: and DIR B:.

The solution is elementary, Watson. Both directories show the same number of files, but the total "bytes free" are different! One disk has, for example, 100352 bytes free, the other has, again an example, only 61440. The difference reveals the existence and size of the hidden files. You've discovered them by deduction... and, of course, subtraction.

If you try this experiment, and the number of "bytes free" don't match my examples, it doesn't matter. The experiment will still solve the Mystery of the Hidden System Files.

Booting With Application Programs

Hidden system files and the COMMAND.COM file must be on a disk in order to boot a computer. That's why, often, the procedure for installing certain application programs includes adding the COMMAND.COM and system files to the PROGRAM DISK...

> **PROGRAM DISK...** the disk of an application program containing the main commands, instructions, and files to run it.

If an application's program disk can boot your computer, it will save you using *both* your DOS disk and your program disk to start work.

> *Make sure the manufacturer of the application directs you to add the system and COMMAND.COM files to the program disk. Sometimes there's not enough room on the disk, or the files on the program disk already inhabit certain sectors that the system needs to function correctly.*

Lets look at two ways to make a "bootable" program disk. The conventional, and easiest, way is to copy the program files onto a "formatted with system" disk.

Unfortunately, this straightforward approach fails if the application's program disk is COPY PROTECTED...

> **COPY PROTECTED...** a disk of files that cannot be accurately copied.

Copy protection prevents you from freely making copies of the application program. If you can't successfully copy the program files onto another disk, and, because the DOS system files are hidden, you can't use the COPY command to copy them onto the program disk.

Of course, it's out of the question to use FORMAT/S on the copy protected disk. That would make the program disk bootable, but all the program files would be gone! The alternative way to make the application program disk bootable is to copy the COMMAND.COM and the system files onto it.

You've already learned how to copy the COMMAND.COM from one disk to another. To copy the hidden systems files requires the SYS command.

The SYS Command

The SYS (SYStem) command is a single purpose version of the COPY command. Not only is it a way to copy the "hidden" system files from the DOS disk to another disk, it's the *only* way.

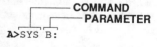

> *Okay. The system files get copied with the DISKCOPY command, too. But everything else on the source disk is included. Not so with the SYS command.*

Try the SYS command now. Put your DOS disk into the A: drive, if it's not already there. Since this is just a practice run, use the disk labelled "BLANK FORMATTED" in the B: drive. The application software's program disk would normally go there. Type **SYS B:**, and press the **[ENTER]** key...

```
        ┌───── COMMAND
     ┌──┼─────── PARAMETER
     │  │
A>SYS B:

System transferred

A> _
```

If you've been following this book in order, and you're using the same version of DOS as I am, you got the message *No room for system on destination disk* (not enough disk space available). All I can say is, "Sorry!"

This is one of those odd things that only technical people understand. Logically, there MUST be room on the target disk because it's a *copy* of all the original files EXCEPT the hidden ones. The reason they won't fit is because DOS system files need *certain sectors* of the disk which are already filled.

System files occupy a unique position on the disk. For example, during formatting, DOS assigns the first track for system files. Most application disks come with this space available. If you copy other files onto a formatted disk, before transferring the system files, the reserved area gets used.

No matter, anyway. This is just practice. Regardless of the success or failure of the system to transfer, you understand the idea.

Once the system files are transferred, all that remains to make the target disk bootable is the COMMAND.COM. If you got the "no room" message, try copying it to the B: drive right now. Type **COPY COMMAND.COM B:**, and press the [ENTER] key...

```
A>COPY COMMAND.COM B:
        1 File(s) copied

A> _
```

It fit on my practice disk, so it no doubt fits on yours, even though there was supposedly no room remaining. There WAS room, just not for the hidden system files.

> *Don't use SYS on application programs unless the manufacturer expressly directs you to do so.*

The Wild Card Filter

You already know that asterisks can be substituted for all the filenames and extensions in a directory. Now see how it can represent parts of filenames or extensions. Begin by typing **COPY A:*.EXE B:**, and pressing the [ENTER] key...

```
           ┌─────── COMMAND
           │   ┌────── SOURCE DRIVE SPECIFIER
           │   │   ┌──────WILD CARD
           │   │   │   ┌──────── SPECIFIED EXTENSION
           │   │   │   │   ┌────────TARGET DRIVE SPECIFIER
           ┌──┐ ┌┐ ┌┐ ┌──┐ ┌┐
A>COPY A:*.EXE B:

A:ATTRIB.EXE
A:FIND.EXE
A:JOIN.EXE
A:SHARE.EXE
A:SORT.EXE
A:SUBST.EXE
        6 File(s) copied

A> _
```

As you can see, the *only* files that copied were those with an EXE extension. This is an example of a FILTER...

FILTER (verb)... *to select and collect from a group by specifying certain criteria.*

By specifying the criterion "all filenames ending with EXE," you filtered the DOS disk of files, allowing only those ending in EXE through.

Now, filter "filenames beginning with the characters BAS." Type **COPY A:BAS*.* B:**...

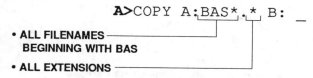

A>COPY A:BAS*.* B: _

- ALL FILENAMES
  BEGINNING WITH BAS
- ALL EXTENSIONS

Press the [ENTER] key...

```
A:BASIC.COM
A:BASICA.COM
        2 File(s) copied

A> _
```

You know that the * character substitutes for any *group* of characters, but what about *single* characters?

The Second Wild Card

The second wild card character, the *?* (question mark), replaces a *single* character. For example, if you want to filter and copy only the DISKCOMP.COM and DISKCOPY.COM files, type **COPY A:DISKCO??.??? B:**...

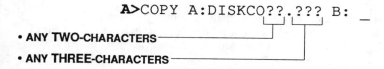

A>COPY A:DISKCO??.??? B: _

- ANY TWO-CHARACTERS
- ANY THREE-CHARACTERS

Press the [ENTER] key...

```
A:DISKCOMP.COM
A:DISKCOPY.COM
        2 File(s) copied

A> _
```

See how the *?* characters found the two files? The *?* wild card is always useful when you want to filter certain words having one or more letters in common, and exclude similar filenames and extensions.

Here are several examples. Each shows how *less specific* criteria makes it likely that extra filenames will turn up. Type **COPY A:M??E.??? B:**...

```
A>COPY A:M??E.???  B:  _
```
• ANY TWO-CHARACTERS
• ANY THREE-CHARACTERS

Press the [ENTER] key...

```
A:MODE.COM
A:MORE.COM
        2 File(s) copied

A>  _
```

Next, type **COPY A:???E.??? B:**, and press the [ENTER] key...

```
A>COPY A:???E.???  B:
A:MODE.COM
A:MORE.COM
A:TREE.COM
        3 File(s) copied

A>  _
```

You picked up one more file. Change the combination by typing **COPY A:?O??.??? B:**, and pressing the [ENTER] key...

```
A>COPY A:?O??.???  B:
A:COMP.COM
A:JOIN.EXE
A:MODE.COM
A:MORE.COM
A:SORT.EXE
        5 File(s) copied

A>  _
```

The extra files show how, occasionally, you may unintentionally filter extra files as the criteria become less specific. For example, if the files DOGS.EAT and MOON.COW were on your practice disk, they'd have copied, too. Accuracy is important.

Inaccurate Use of Wild Cards

If you try to copy a file that *isn't* there, DOS comments...

```
A>COPY A:NOFILE.*  B:
A:NOFILE.??? File not found
        0 File(s) copied

A>  _
```

Or, suppose you want all files with two-character extensions. Type
COPY A:????.?? B:...

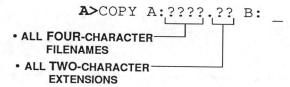

A>COPY A:????.?? B: _

• ALL FOUR-CHARACTER
    FILENAMES

• ALL TWO-CHARACTER
    EXTENSIONS

Press the [**ENTER**] key...

```
Volume in drive A has no label
Directory of A:\

File not found

A> _
```

There are no two-character extensions on the master DOS disk, so no file was found.

> *REMEMBER: When specifying files, make certain spelling is accurate. Include extensions. And, specify appropriate drive parameters.*

Wild DIR and DEL Commands

Both wild card characters work with the DIR (DIRectory) and the ERASE or DEL (DELete) commands. With these commands, you can *selectively* look at a directory of files, or get rid of a batch of files simultaneously.

Experiment. Try some of the previous wild card COPY examples substituting DIR, ERASE, or DEL. Be careful with DEL.

Permanently Gone

I will now accent the obvious. When you ERASE, or DEL, one or more files, that's it! The data's gone. This finality is so important that when wild cards are in use, DOS issues a warning.

Type **DEL B:*.***, and press the [**ENTER**] key...

```
A>DEL B:*.*
Are you sure (Y / N)?

A> _
```

See? A last chance warning. Type **N**, and press the **[ENTER]** key to get safely back to the system prompt with no harm done.

Comforting? Well, unfortunately, DOS gives this last chance warning for "all files" only. If you specify one file or filter a batch, DOS gives no warning!

> *When you erase a file, DOS doesn't really erase it. It only modifies the directory. There are software programs on the market with which you can change the directory back. This is called UNERASING. The unerasing usually fails if any new files have been added to the disk since the erase.*
>
> *Just thought I'd mention this. It may come in handy some day.*

COPY Command Precautions

As you now know, to copy a file from one directory to another is simply a matter of giving the command, the filename, and specifying the source and target. The reason you specify the source and target is because DOS has some rules about filenames and extensions. For example, DOS won't let you copy a file onto itself. Try it by typing **COPY COMMAND.COM**, and pressing the **[ENTER]** key...

```
A>COPY COMMAND.COM
File cannot be copied onto itself
     0 File(s) copied

A> _
```

The reason for this message is that DOS only allows one file with the same filename and extension per directory. How, then, you might ask, were you able to repeatedly copy the same files onto the disk in the B: drive? By now that disk must have *several* copies of the same files. Well, look at the directory.

As you can see, there are no duplicates. The reason our continuous copying hasn't added any additional files is OVERWRITE...

> **OVERWRITE...** *to write data onto data.*

If you copy a file from one disk to another, and the source and target *filenames and extensions* are identical, the source file *overwrites* the target file. The new data replaces the old. The purpose is to get the most economical use of disk space. This benefit can become a catastrophe, though, if you accidentally overwrite a file.

This type of accident occurs when filenames are too similar. Too similar means they can be mistaken or forgotten, then used in error. Since this type of oversight can hardly be avoided over a long period of time, take precautions. The simplest is to check the existing filenames on the target disk.

AVOID ACCIDENTALLY OVERWRITING FILES

Before using the COPY command, use the DIR command to check the filenames on the target disk.

Check spelling, too. Similar spelling of files can be risky.

Testing Write Protection

In chapter eight, you write protected your master DOS disk so no files could be destroyed. Do the same with your working copy.

Now try to copy all the files from the B: drive onto this write protected disk in the A: drive. Type **COPY B:*.* A:**, and press the **[ENTER]** key...

```
A>COPY B:*.* A:
B:ANSI.SYS

Write protect error writing drive A
Abort, Retry, Ignore?

A> _
```

Type A to abort. (If you want to see what happens with "retry" and "ignore," go ahead.)

Always write protect disks containing files you don't want to accidentally lose.

Change A Filename With COPY

What if you *want* two copies of the same file on the same disk? You know that two files with the same name can't exist on the same directory. So, if you want duplicate files, they must have *different* names.

One way to manage it is to use the COPY command to change a file's name. Here's how easy it is. Type **COPY A:COMMAND.COM B:NEWNAME**, and press the [ENTER] key...

```
A>COPY A:COMMAND.COM B:NEWNAME
        1 File(s) copied

A> _
```

• **TARGET DRIVE
    AND NEW FILENAME**

Simultaneously, DOS copies and changes the name of a file. The file called NEWNAME that just arrived on the disk in the B: drive is a duplicate COMMAND.COM file. You now have two copies of the same file on the same disk, only the names differ.

By changing the name of a file, you can copy any number of duplicates onto any directory. Just remember to follow the rules of specifying sources and targets.

WARNING

When you COPY and change filenames, watch that you don't send a file to the wrong drive! You could lose track of it.

Okay. Now it's clear that you can have more than one copy of the same file by renaming it *as you copy it*. Most often, though, you don't want a copy, just a new name. For that, DOS provides the RENAME command.

The RENAME Command

The RENAME, or REN (REName), command does just what it says, and that all. It will change a file's name, but it won't change its location.

Try it now to get the idea. Type **REN B:COMMAND.COM NEWNAME2**, and press the [ENTER] key...

```
A>REN B:COMMAND.COM NEWNAME2

A> _
```

Did anything happen? Look at the directory of the B: drive. To anyone not knowing what you did, the COMMAND.COM is gone. Actually, NEWNAME2 *is* the COMMAND.COM file – with a new name.

Remember, you can RENAME a file, but this command will not affect its location. Type **REN B:NEWNAME2 A:COMMAND.COM**, and press the **[ENTER]** key...

```
A>REN B:NEWNAME2 A:COMMAND.COM
Invalid parameter

A> _
```

As you can see, something didn't work. DOS has given you an error message, *Invalid parameter.*

> *If you're using some version of DOS earlier than 3.1, the message won't appear, and the file's name will change. Under no version, however, will the file's location change.*

Supplemental Ways To Use The COPY Command

The COPY command can also be used in conjunction with a DEVICE...

> **DEVICE...** *computerese for hardware such as keyboard, monitor, or printer. It's a synonym of another computerese term: PERIPHERAL.*

You can use a device, by name, just as you would a filename. Here are the principle devices and their names...

Devices	*Names of Devices*
Keyboard & Monitor	*CON*
Printers	*LPT1, LPT2, LPT3, PRN*
Mouse & Modem	*AUX, COM1, COM2*

CON (CONsole), for example, which is computerese for the basic input and output devices of a computer system, is the device you use most. The CON input is the keyboard. The CON output is the monitor, or display screen.

Now we're going to use the CON device to interface (I use that word every chance I get) other devices and the disk operating system.

The SCROLL.TXT File

You're going to use CON and the COPY command to make a text file (that's a file full of text). This file will be the vehicle for trying out the devices.

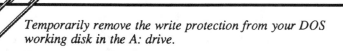

> *Temporarily remove the write protection from your DOS working disk in the A: drive.*

Clear your screen of everything but the system prompt to avoid any confusion. Just type **CLS** (CLear Screen), and press the [**ENTER**] key. Then, carefully follow the next instructions.

First, tell DOS to "COPY from the CONsole a file called SCROLL.TXT" by typing **COPY CON SCROLL.TXT**, and pressing the [**ENTER**] key...

```
A>COPY CON SCROLL.TXT
_
```

Second, put some text into the file by typing the sentence **THIS IS A LINE**...

```
A>COPY CON SCROLL.TXT
THIS IS A LINE_
```

Press the [**ENTER**] key...

```
A>COPY CON SCROLL.TXT
THIS IS A LINE
_
```

Now the easy way to type, press the **F3** key...

```
A>COPY CON SCROLL.TXT
THIS IS A LINE
THIS IS A LINE_
```

How about that?! The **F3** key retypes THIS IS A LINE. Press the [**ENTER**] key and the F3 key again to get to the next line.

Press the **F3** key and [**ENTER**] keys at least thirty more times. Yes, that's right, THIRTY TIMES.

Finally, press the **F6** key (or type **^Z**), followed by the **[ENTER]** key...

```
THIS IS A LINE
THIS IS A LINE
THIS IS A LINE
THIS IS A LINE
THIS IS A LINE
THIS IS A LINE
^Z
        1 File(s) copied

A> _
```

DOS takes over. It copies this information from the CONsole onto the disk in the logged drive, creating a file, and naming it SCROLL.TXT!

> *If you make a mistake, cancel the procedure by pressing the [CTRL] and C keys. Type CLS, and press the [ENTER] key. Then begin again.*

Check to see if the file's there with the DIR command. I'll assume it's there. Then check to see if the contents are there. How? The COPY command again.

Looking Inside A File

The best way to look inside text files is with a word processor. But, when you're in a rush, perhaps searching through several files for some general information, here's a handy shortcut.

Begin at the system prompt. Type **COPY A:SCROLL.TXT CON**, and press the **[ENTER]** key...

```
A>COPY A:SCROLL.TXT CON
THIS IS A LINE
THIS IS A LINE
THIS IS A LINE
THIS IS A LINE




THIS IS A LINE
THIS IS A LINE
THIS IS A LINE
THIS IS A LINE
        1 File(s) copied

A>_
```

Your screen fills with the contents of the A:SCROLL.TXT file because you told DOS to "copy the SCROLL.TXT file onto the screen."

> *Because you made this file longer than twenty-four lines, it scrolls by before you can read it. You can stop the scrolling of any file with the [CTRL] S command. This is explained on page 33.*

Besides helping you take quick peeks when looking for some particular information, this technique is one quick way to solve the recurring "Mystery of the Cryptic Filename." When the name of a file doesn't give a clue to its content, you COPY it to CON, and see what's what!

Other Devices As Targets

Now to COPY a file to the device called PRN...

> **PRN...** *means default printer. When your computer system is set up, the default PRN is specifically LPT1, LPT2, or LPT3. LPT1 means Line PrinTer 1. DOS supports three line, commonly called parallel, printers. (Serial printers use the COM1 or COM2 outputs.)*

Make sure your printer's on, then type **COPY A:SCROLL.TXT PRN**, and press the [ENTER] key...

```
A>COPY A:SCROLL.TXT PRN
            1 File(s) copied

A> _
```

As soon as you enter this instruction, it's obvious what you told DOS to do. And, your printer responds accordingly.

By the way, don't expect classy formatting (margins, tabs, bold type, under-lining, etc.) when copying from a file to a device, the CON or the PRN. To make text presentable, you need an application program such as a word processor.

Finally...

So, at last, we come to the end of this long chapter. If you wearied along the way, take comfort in the fact that, while learning the COPY command, you also learned some subtleties of the DIR, RENAME (REN), and ERASE (DEL) commands. You discovered the SYS command, too. That's FIVE for the price of ONE!

We're not through with the COPY command, though. There's a critical use for it which gets an entire chapter – the next one.

10 *BACK UP*

No, we're not going to start over. BACK UP means to make a copy. A BACKUP, two words as one, *is* a copy. Sometimes, the hyphenated approach appears in print – BACK-UP! I don't know what that one means.

I use the two word version, BACK UP, as a verb; the single word, BACKUP, as a noun. "You should BACK UP often by making BACKUPS."

Back Up and Backup

Electronic media, which includes disks, are vulnerable. Perhaps the safest way to protect one is to print its contents on paper – known in computerese as a HARD COPY. If your backup is a hard copy, though, further processing would mean reentering the data – definitely a slow process. The preferable approach is the well established disk backup.

A disk backup is simply saving a copy of data from one disk onto another. Why not, then, call it SAVE?

To SAVE Is To Back Up

Simply put, save is synonymous with back up. The term "save" is used interchangeably with backup in reference to copying a file from RAM before turning off the computer. As you know, when the computer goes off, the data in RAM goes away. That's why frequent saving during work sessions with application programs is a good policy. And, most modern application programs keep data in RAM during work sessions.

The reason I bring this up is that many application programs have built in functions for saving work files. No DOS command such as COPY command is needed.

For example, imagine you're writing a letter with a word processing program. After a few paragraphs, you SAVE your work using the "save" command...

LETTER.DOC

The saved file is called, in our example,
LETTER.DOC. The DOC stands for
DOCument. You continue your work, adding
a few paragraphs to the letter. You save
again...

LETTER.BAK
LETTER.DOC

The result is two files, the one you saved first plus the one you just saved.
The word processor gives each of these files a different extension to
differentiate them, and because DOS doesn't allow two files with the same
name in a directory.

The most recent file saved gets the DOC extension. The previous file saved
automatically gets a new extension. In our example, it's BAK for BAcKup.
In a way, you could say there are now TWO backups. One backs up RAM;
the other backs up the original save.

As you continue adding to your letter, and
periodically saving, the process continues.
No matter how many times you save,
though, only the *last two* files are available
on the disk directory. Earlier versions are
erased...

CURRENT SAVES OF
LETTER.DOC and LETTTER.BAK

The illustration shows how DOS uses
available space when it writes onto a disk.
The result of repeated editing is data scattered
over the surface of the disk...

Gradually, your computer slows slightly as
DOS collects, organizes, and reorganizes   TOO MANY SCATTERED BITS
thousands of bits and bytes. You may not
notice the gradual decrease in speed with the newest application programs and
processors. But, if you do, it might remind you that the data is becoming
dangerously scattered. Scattered data increases the risk of losing a file. For
safety's sake, make a backup disk.

The Backup Disk

The routinely recommended procedure for making a backup disk is to use the DISKCOPY command, resulting in...

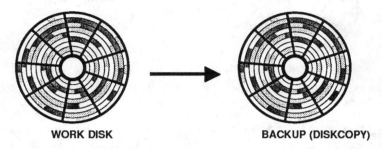

WORK DISK   BACKUP (DISKCOPY)

Comparing the original with the backup, you see the files scattered on BOTH. Is there a better way? There is.

You can check, or eliminate, the scattering by copying the *files* rather than the *disk*. Copy them onto a blank, formatted disk using COPY *.*. With this method, DOS organizes and lays down all the parts of the files in contiguous (side by side) blocks...

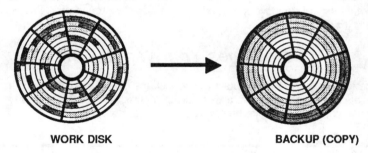

WORK DISK   BACKUP (COPY)

At this point, the accepted procedure is to put away the backup in case of trouble, making it safe to continue to work. But, is that the right way? Does it make sense to continue working with a disk full of scattered files?

No. The better choice is the opposite. Do it backwards.

The Backward Backup

I call this tactic the BACKWARD BACKUP because it's the opposite of the accepted procedure, and because it's an alliteration. There's no procedural difference except the labelling. The disks are the same as in the previous illustration. Only the labels are changed...

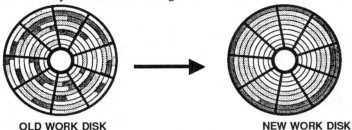

OLD WORK DISK   **NEW WORK DISK**

The *original* becomes the file copy – the backup. Put *it* away. Use the *copy* as the new work disk.

The BACKWARD BACKUP approach gives you an improved work medium that responds faster. It reduces the risk of lost material through data error, too. Data error is the principle culprit leading to a situation called a CRASH...

> **CRASH...** *inside the computer all the electrons get confused or angry and go on strike. DOS gets stuck. The computer stops computing, and you've got trouble.*

The definition may not be *technically* correct, but the result's the same. The only memory of your work will be what you backed up on disk, the backup. The rest will be gone.

Sometimes You Want It Gone

Occasionally, as you accumulate many backups, you may find it expedient to ERASE irrelevant files from a work disk. You get rid of files, not only because you no longer need them, but to recover disk space.

> *TIP: Get extra room on your work disk by copying only the files you want when you make a Backward Backup. For example, copy only the DOC files. Don't bother with the BAK files.*

Just don't forget that an ERASE operation is permanent. Avoid accidental erasing by taking the time to carefully label all disks. Date them, too. Use bold print on labels whenever you have enough room. Colored ink, colored labels, or both, are available now. Sentinel Technologies markets high quality disks with brightly colored jackets. Check them out.

Remember this – you may only have a few disks now, and can't imagine accumulating an excessive number of disks, files, and backups. You will. And, you've been warned.

11 THE ESSENTIAL ELEVEN

If you're someone who's been struggling with DOS for a while, picked up this book and flipped to this chapter for some quick answers, perhaps that's okay. Perhaps this is the only chapter you need. But, if you want to quickly and easily learn the essentials of DOS, and stop that struggling, I recommend you read this book from the beginning.

If you've completed the previous chapters, you're almost finished learning all the DOS you'll probably ever need. From now on, whenever you need some reminders of what you've learned, look here first.

As I explained at the beginning of this book, the "Essential Eleven" are the routine and repetitive DOS operations you *need to know* to use a floppy disk personal computer.

Here are the Essential Eleven in brief...

DOS commands are either INTERNAL or EXTERNAL.

INTERNAL commands automatically load into RAM when you boot the computer. They're **inside** the computer. These commands are always available at the system prompt. Internal is also called MEMORY RESIDENT.

EXTERNAL commands are **outside** the computer – on the DOS disk. To use these commands from the system prompt, the DOS disk must be in a drive.

1. DATE
(See chapter six)

An internal command. At the system prompt, you can use this command to check or change the current date.

2. TIME
(See chapter six)

An internal command. At the system prompt, you can use this command to check or change the current time.

3. DIR
(See chapters seven and nine)

An internal command. At the system prompt, you can use this command to see a list of the files of a disk in any drive.

(Use WILD CARDS to filter for specific files.)

(DIR/P will PAUSE a scrolling directory. DIR/W will show filenames and extensions only.)

4. CHKDSK
(See Addendum)

An external command. At the system prompt, you can use this utility program to check a disk for the amount of used and available space. It also shows the amount of used and available RAM.

5. FORMAT
(See chapter eight)

An external command. At the system prompt, you can use this utility program to have DOS analyze a new or used disk for defective tracks, initialize a directory, set up file allocations, and make other technical modifications in preparation for storing files.

(FORMAT/S adds COMMAND.COM and hidden system files.)

Some computer systems use the term INITIALIZE which is basically the same function as formatting.

6. DISKCOPY
(See chapter eight)

An external command. At the system prompt, you can use this command to make a duplicate of any disk. DISKCOPY also formats blank disks before copying.

(DISKCOPY A: B: copies from one drive to another.)

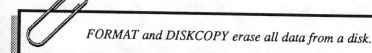

FORMAT and DISKCOPY erase all data from a disk.

7. DISKCOMP
(See chapter eight)

An external command. At the system prompt, you can use this command to compare two disks sector by sector. DISKCOMP will only recognize exact duplicates as "ok."

(DISKCOMP A: B: compares disks in two drives.)

8. COPY
(See chapter nine)

An internal command. At the system prompt, you can use this command to copy one or more files to or from disks and devices. While copying, you can also change filenames and combine files.

(Use the WILD CARD characters, the * and the ? to save time.)

9. ERASE or DEL
(See chapter nine)

An internal command. At the system prompt, you can use this command to erase one or more files. NOTE: You can substitute DEL (DELete) for ERASE. DOS recognizes either.

(Use WILD CARDS to ERASE several files at once.)

10. RENAME or REN
(See chapter nine)

An internal command. At the system prompt, you can use this command to change a file's name. NOTE: Save yourself three keystrokes by using REN instead of RENAME.

11. SYS
(See chapter nine and the Addendum)

An external command. At the system prompt, you can copy the DOS system files from the DOS disk.

That's them... "The Essential Eleven."

For some additional relevant details and tips, turn to the ADDENDUM.

ADDENDUM

Here are important ideas and tips you'll need from time to time. You won't need them often, but when you do, they're indispensable.

Specifying Drives

No sooner do I proclaim this addendum to contain items you won't use often, I present one that you will. It's a leftover from chapter nine which was so long, I held out this technique with the COPY, DIR, and ERASE commands. It's a typing shortcut.

When you don't specify a drive, DOS uses the logged drive. Therefore, the simplest way to enter these parameters is to not enter them. In other words, don't specify the logged drive, since DOS uses it anyway.

Here are some examples of parameters without typing the logged drive...

Standard	Simplified
A>COPY A:SCROLL.TXT B:	A>COPY SCROLL.TXT B:
A>COPY A:*.* B:	A>COPY *.* B:
A>COPY B:SCROLL.TXT A:	A>COPY B:SCROLL.TXT
A>ERASE A:*.TXT	A>ERASE *.TXT
A>DIR A:	A>DIR

In case you don't see the differences between Standard and Simplified, look at the A: parameters in the first column. Then look to see they're not in the second. Even without the parameter to specify the logged drive, these instructions are identical.

Panic! Cancel!

In chapter seven, you used [CTRL] S (CTRL meaning the CONTROL key) to stop and start a scrolling screen. Sometimes, though, you won't want to continue a scroll at all. You'll want to forget it. Use [CTRL] C. It's a "panic" command meaning CANCEL.

[CTRL] [BREAK] does the same thing. It means "BREAK OFF" or "Put on the BRAKES." (I invented the last two definitions.)

Here's an example of "cancelling" or "breaking off" a scrolling directory, and returning to the system prompt. Try cancelling a scrolling screen right now with either method. Begin by typing **DIR**, and pressing the [**ENTER**] key...

```
A>DIR

Volume in drive A has no label
Directory of  A:\

ANSI     SYS     1651   3-07-85   1:43p
ASSIGN   COM     1509   3-07-85   1:43p
ATTRIB   EXE    15091   3-07-85   1:43p
BACKUP   COM     5577   3-07-85   1:43p
BASIC    COM    17792   3-07-85   1:43p
BASICA   COM    27520   3-07-85   1:43p
CHKDSK   COM      94^C
 —
```
BREAKING OFF

When the break occurs, a ^C appears. The ^ represents the [**CTRL**] key.

Which DOS Version?

When using disks from other computers, certain DOS commands may give you the message *Wrong DOS version.* This means you're trying to use a DOS command on a disk that's incompatible with the version used to boot the system.

Which version of DOS is in use? At the system prompt, type **VER**, and press the [**ENTER**] key. DOS will tell you.

To match disk and DOS, copy the files from the problem disk onto a disk formatted for the DOS version you're using.

Diagnostics

Hardware manufacturers provide DIAGNOSTIC software with DOS. Sometimes it's a disk separate from your DOS disk. Sometimes it's just a file on your DOS disk called TEST. Whatever comes with your hardware, this is an important DOS external utility because it will check your entire computer system for you. Use it to make certain that everything you bought is there, and it all works.

Your computer manual will provide you with the information you need to start a diagnosis. After that, the step-by-step instructions on the screen are invariably easy to follow. In all the DIAGNOSTIC and TEST programs I've tried, the only term I found that might be puzzling is a screen prompt for a "scratch disk." This is merely computerese meaning "a disk that you don't mind erasing."

The CHKDSK Command

Try CHKDSK (CHecK DiSK), one of the "Essential Eleven" DOS commands, to check the DOS disk in the A: drive. Type **CHKDSK**...

```
A>CHKDSK _
```

Then press the **[ENTER]** key...

```
362496 bytes total disk space  <——————— DISK STORAGE OF LOGGED DRIVE
 38912 bytes in 3 hidden files <——— Space used by SYSTEM files
264192 bytes in 37 user files  <——— Space used by files
 59392 bytes available on disk  <——— Remaining space on disk

655360 bytes total memory <——— Total RAM
630784 bytes free  <——————————— Available RAM

A> _
```

> NOTE: THE 37TH FILE IS "SCROLL.TXT"

This is how CHKDSK checks the logged drive. To check a disk in the B: drive, use a drive specifying parameter. Just type **CHKDSK B:**, and press the **[ENTER]** key. Or, log onto that drive by typing **B:**. Then enter the CHKDSK command without a parameter.

If you intend to use CHKDSK to routinely check disk and memory limits, copy it from the DOS disk onto any application disk you'll be routinely using. Don't worry if you don't feel an immediate need to do this. I've never done it, but one associate of mine considers it an essential precaution.

Two DOS "Goodies"

Two DOS "goodies" are CONFIG.SYS and AUTOEXEC.BAT. Each apparently fits under the heading of "Technical Areas To Avoid." BUT, these two files are especially helpful and easy to use.

Either you make these files, they come with an application, or you get someone to make them for you when needed. Whichever way, you benefit. DOS takes care of that.

CONFIG.SYS is a special file of instructions that modifies the operation of certain commands and devices. Some application programs require such a file.

That's all you *need* to know about CONFIG.SYS. That's all I know about it, and I've used most of the popular application programs on the market.

AUTOEXEC.BAT is a file that "AUTOmatically EXECutes a BATch of commands." Batch, believe it or not, is computerese for a list or group. I guess batch was someone's idea of "friendly." Maybe it was the guy who came up with boot?!

Anyway, an AUTOEXEC.BAT file works in one of two ways. The first is when the computer is booted. DOS searches for the COMMAND.COM file, then searches for any file called AUTOEXEC.BAT to get special instructions. If it finds such a file, it "automatically executes the batch" in it.

The second way to use an AUTOEXEC.BAT file is from the system prompt. Type **AUTOEXEC**, and press the **[ENTER]** key. No need to include the BAT.

Whenever you add or modify a CONFIG.SYS or AUTOEXEC.BAT file, reboot your computer to instruct DOS that operational changes have been made.

PrtSc

[SHIFT] **[PrtSc]** is the PRinT Screen command. It's on your keyboard to the right.

Press either of the **[SHIFT]** keys, and the **[PrtSc]** key. The display on your screen will print. Computerese for this is SCREEN DUMP. Classy, huh?

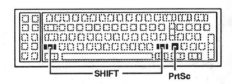

[CTRL] **[PrtSc]** will send all characters that appear on your screen to your printer. Press these keys again to turn off this function. Who knows, maybe this will be useful to you sometime?!

MORE HARDWARE

A few additional pieces of hardware can make your computer more versatile and easier to use...

More RAM

Depending on the application programs you're using, or intend to use, your computer may need more RAM. Not long ago, 64k of RAM was enough for most personal computers to run most programs. Times have changed. Look at the labels of the commercial programs you intend to use. The minimum amount of RAM needed is clearly marked. If you're starting out today, I recommend *at least* 512k. Better, 640k!

A Built-In Clock

If you're like me, you hate to type the date and time when booting. Do what I did. Get a built-in, crystal controlled clock and calendar with battery backup. Mine came with the extra RAM board which I added to get 640k in my computer.

Hard Disk

If you want enough static memory to do about anything, get a HARD DISK. A hard disk is capable of holding ALL your programs and working data. A hard disk can remember 10 million (MEGA) bytes or more! When you switch on the computer, all your software can be immediately available.

Well, it's not THAT easy. For example, hard disks can forget everything if a mechanical problem turns up. And, the "Essential Eleven" are eight commands short if you're running a hard disk. See *Hard DOS It!* for easy ways to learn how to use a hard disk, and the "Easy Eight."

Oh, yeah. A hard disk is usually called the C: drive.

Do You Need The MODE Command?

The MODE command affects the communication PORTS...

> **PORT...** *an output plug from a slot in the rear or side of a computer.*

The communication ports are COM1: and COM2:. The types of hardware you'll most likely use these for are serial printer, MOUSE, or MODEM.

Printers are either parallel or serial. Parallel printers use the LPT ports, as explained in chapter nine. Serial printers use the communication ports.

A MOUSE is a mechanical adjunct to the keyboard. It's a device for moving the cursor on the screen, or otherwise substituting for keyboard commands, that's operated by hand on some horizontal surface.

A MODEM is a telecommunications device. It can be internal or external. The terms MODE and MODEM aren't directly related. MODE, as you know, is a DOS command. MODEM is a combined form of the words MODulate and DEModulate. Computerese can be as tricky as the rest of our language. So be on guard.

For more about modems, refer to *The EASY MODEM & FAX Book* by Ron Bauer.

That's all. The rest is... EASY!